JAN 0 8 2015

W9-AXI-083

Road Safety

Road Safety

Christie Marlowe

Mason Crest

Allen County Public Library

Mason Crest
450 Parkway Drive, Suite D
Broomall, PA 19008
www.masoncrest.com

Copyright © 2015 by Mason Crest, an imprint of National Highlights, Inc. All rights reserved. No part of this publication may be reproduced or transmitted in any form or by any means, electronic or mechanical, including photocopying, recording, taping, or any information storage and retrieval system, without permission from the publisher.

Printed and bound in the United States of America.

First printing
9 8 7 6 5 4 3 2 1

Series ISBN: 978-1-4222-3044-2
ISBN: 978-1-4222-3052-7
ebook ISBN: 978-1-4222-8836-8

Library of Congress Cataloging-in-Publication Data

Marlowe, Christie.
  Road safety / Christie Marlowe.
      pages cm. – (Safety first)
  Includes index.
  Audience: Ages 10+
  Audience: Grade 4 to 6.
  ISBN 978-1-4222-3044-2 (series)—ISBN 978-1-4222-3052-7 (hardback)—ISBN 978-1-4222-8836-8 (ebook) 1. Traffic safety–Juvenile literature. 2. Pedestrians–Safety measures–Juvenile literature. 3. Safety education–Juvenile literature. I. Title.
  HE5614.M298 2015
  363.12'5–dc23
                              2014003853

Contents

Introduction

No task is more important than creating safe schools for all children. It should not require an act of courage for parents to send their children to school nor for children to come to school. As adults, we must do everything reasonable to provide a school climate that is safe, secure, and welcoming—an environment where learning can flourish. The educational effectiveness and the strength of any nation is dependent upon a strong and effective educational system that empowers and prepares young people for meaningful and purposeful lives that will promote economic competitiveness, national defense, and quality of life.

Clearly adults are charged with the vital responsibility of creating a positive educational climate. However, the success of young people is also affected by their own participation. The purpose of this series of books is to articulate what young adults can do to ensure their own safety, while at the same time educating them as to the steps that educators, parents, and communities are taking to create and maintain safe schools. Each book in the series gives young people tools that will empower them as participants in this process. The result is a model where students have the information they need to work alongside parents, educators, and community leaders to tackle the safety challenges that face young people every day.

Perhaps one of the most enduring and yet underrated challenges facing young adults is bullying. Ask parents if they can remember the schoolyard bully from when they were in school, and the answers are quite revealing. Unfortunately, the situation is no better today—and new venues for bullying exist in the twenty-first-century world that never existed before. A single bully can intimidate not only a single student but an entire classroom, an entire school, and even an entire community. The problem is underscored by research from the National School Safety Center and the United States Secret Service that indicates that bullying was involved in 80 percent of school shootings over the past two decades. The title in this series that addresses this problem is a valuable and essential tool for promoting safety and stopping bullying.

Another problem that has been highlighted by the media is the threat of violence on our school campuses. In reality, research tells us that schools are the safest place for young people to be. After an incident like Columbine or Sandy Hook, however, it is difficult for the public, including students, to understand that a youngster is a hundred times more likely to be assaulted or killed at home or in the community than at school. Students cannot help but absorb the fears that are so prevalent in our society. Therefore, a frank, realistic, discussion of this topic, one that avoids hysteria and exaggeration, is essential for our young people. This series offers a title on this topic that does exactly that. It addresses questions such as: How do you deal with a gunman on the campus? Should you run, hide, or confront? We do not want to scare our children; instead, we want to empower them and reassure them as we prepare them for such a crisis. The book also covers the changing laws and school policies that are being put in place to ensure that students are even safer from the threat of violence in the school.

"Stranger danger" is another safety threat that receives a great deal of attention in the modern world. Again, the goal should be to empower rather than terrify our children. The book in this series focusing on this topic provides young readers with the essential information that will help them be "safety smart," not only at school but also between home and school, at play, and even when they are home alone.

Alcohol and drug abuse is another danger that looms over our young people. As many as 10 percent of American high school students are alcoholics. Meanwhile, when one student was asked, "Is there a drug problem in your school?" her reply was, "No, I can get all the drugs I want." A book in this series focuses on this topic, giving young readers the information they need to truly comprehend that drugs and alcohol are major threats to their safety and well-being.

From peer pressure to natural disasters, from road dangers to sports safety, the Safety First series covers a wide range of other modern concerns. Keeping children and our schools safe is not an isolated challenge. It will require all of us working together to create a climate where young people can have safe access to the educational opportunities that will promote the success of all children as they transition into becoming responsible citizens. This series is an essential tool for classrooms, libraries, guidance counselors, and community centers as they face this challenge.

Dr. Ronald Stephens
Executive Director
National School Safety Center
www.schoolsafety.us

Words to Know

suburban: Outside the city.
unconscious: Not awake and aware, sometimes due to an injury, accident, or health issue.

Chapter One

Real-Life Stories

Alex started riding a bicycle when he was only five years old. He even remembers the day he learned to ride without his training wheels—the speed, the wind blowing past his face. That was a very special day. For Alex, it meant that he finally had some freedom. He no longer had to rely on his mom to get him from one place to another. A little bit of the road was finally his. But what Alex didn't know was that if we don't put our safety first, the road can be a very dangerous place.

ALEX AND SUBURBAN ROADS

Growing up in a **suburban** town was, in some ways, really great. Alex's school was big, which meant that he had a lot of friends in his neighborhood, and his home had a big yard, which gave him a lot of space to play. But as he grew older, Alex didn't only want to stay at home. And having to ask his mom for rides when he wanted to go to the store or to a friend's house was annoying. In a city, Alex wouldn't always need his mom if he wanted to leave the house. People who live in cities have many ways to get around—taxis, buses, and trains, for example—and things are so close together in a city that a lot of places are within walking distance. Safety around roads in the city is also very important, but we'll talk more about that more later.

9

Bikes can be a great way to get around, but they can also be dangerous. Make sure you respect traffic laws and be careful around cars whenever you're biking on the road.

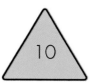

Road Safety

Even if you're not driving, you have to be aware of traffic laws and the cars around you. Roads can be very dangerous, so it's important to be aware of traffic.

Walking around his neighborhood was a pretty safe way to travel if Alex made sure to look both ways before crossing the street and to stay aware of the cars and people around him. But it was also tiring and difficult. Sometimes he and his friends would take long walks down to the local grocery store or over to the next neighborhood to visit friends. But if he wanted to go any further, he had to ask his mom for a ride—or ride his bike.

ALEX IGNORES THE RULES OF THE ROAD

Alex always loved his bike. Once his mom finally let him travel further than a few streets from his house, Alex always seemed to be on his bike. He rode it to school, to stores, to visit friends, to the local park, and to play sports with his friends.

All of his riding worried his mom. There are a lot of cars on the road, and she was scared that Alex wasn't staying safe. She told him all she could about staying safe on the road. She told Alex

Many cities are designed for pedestrians and bicycles to get around easily, whereas suburban areas are spaced farther apart, so people often need a car to get around.

Road Safety

It can be very dangerous to be biking on the road. In an accident between a bicycle and a car, the bike rider is much more likely to get hurt.

cyclists must follow the same rules drivers follow. She told him always to ride on the right side of the road. In many cities, there is a lane set aside for bikers. But in the suburbs, there usually isn't a separate lane for people riding their bikes. Alex's mom told him to make sure he stayed far enough to the side of the road that he wouldn't be in the way of traffic. She told him to always stop at stop signs and red lights, and to be extra careful at railroad crossings. She told Alex to make sure he used a hand signal whenever crossing the street or making a turn. She made sure that his bike had four reflectors—one on the front, one on the back, and one on each wheel—for riding after dark. Reflectors are anything shiny that reflects light. When the light from a car hits them, they light up so that the driver in the car can see them. Most important, she made sure he always wore his helmet and wore it properly.

Alex mostly ignored his mom's warnings, however. He rarely stopped at stop signs or red lights. He seldom used hand signals. Sometimes, after leaving the house, he would take off his helmet

The best way to avoid head injuries from a bike accident is to wear a helmet. It can be tempting not to, but if you're biking, you should always wear your helmet!

Road Safety

What Are Hand Signals?

When you make arm motions while riding your bike to let cars and other bikers know what you are about to do, you are using hand signals. Since a bike rider should always ride on the right side of the road, hand signals are always made with your left arm. A left turn is signaled by sticking your arm straight out beside you. When you hold your left arm up, bent at the elbow, you're telling others you're going to make a right turn. When you want to slow down or stop, stick your left arm down toward the ground.

and ride with it around his handlebars. He knew in his state, it was illegal for someone under the age of eighteen to ride a bike without wearing a helmet. But many of the other boys rode without their helmets, and the risk of being caught by a police officer just added to the thrill.

Alex thought following these rules was a waste of time. There were never too many cars on the roads in his neighborhood. He was sure he could stay safe enough just by staying aware of the cars and cyclists that shared the roads with him. He never considered the rules were made for a very important reason and that ignoring them could be extremely dangerous.

ALEX GETS INTO AN ACCIDENT

One hot summer day, Alex was invited over to a friend's house to swim in the pool. The house was in another neighborhood. It wasn't a long bike ride, but there were some very busy roads between Alex's house and his friend's house. His mom offered to give him a ride in her car. But Alex told his mom he wanted to ride his bike. She told him he couldn't go unless she drove him. Instead of playing it safe, he lied to her and told her he didn't want to go anymore. He told her he was going to ride his bike to visit a friend in the neighborhood. Alex told her he wouldn't go near the busy roads. Unfortunately, this was a lie Alex and his mom would never forget.

Alex left the house wearing his helmet, like he always did. But when he met up with Ethan, one of his neighbors, he quickly took off his helmet and tied it to his handlebars. The busy roads scared Alex, but he didn't want Ethan to think he was afraid. In truth, Ethan was just as scared as Alex was. But he, too, didn't want to look scared in front of Alex. And the thought of relaxing in their friend's pool was enough to make them risk the dangerous ride over there.

The main roads seemed especially busy that day. The cars passed Ethan and Alex very quickly. Ethan was riding ahead of Alex, and Alex pedaled quickly to keep up. Ethan was a few years older than Alex, and Alex wanted his respect. He didn't want Ethan to view him as too young or as a weakling who couldn't keep up with him.

The boys were finally nearing their friend's neighborhood. They needed to cross the road to get there. Ethan looked both ways and made a split-second decision to cross. He was able to make it across safely. But Alex wasn't so lucky. Instead of looking both ways or using any hand signals, he quickly followed Ethan, without stopping to consider whether it was safe to cross the road.

Real-Life Stories

15

In 2011, 677 bicyclists were killed in traffic accidents, and many more were injured. When you're biking, make sure you take every precaution to be safe.

Road Safety

A car nearly hit him head-on but was able to turn at the last second, and ended up hitting Alex's back tire. Alex was thrown off his bike and hit his head on the curb. Because he wasn't wearing his helmet, the blow to his head was very powerful. Ethan saw the crash and ran over to see if Alex was OK. The person who hit Alex pulled over. Seeing that Alex was **unconscious** and that his head was bleeding, the driver called an ambulance. The ambulance was there in minutes and quickly rushed Alex to the hospital.

Alex got a concussion and broke his arm in the crash. A concussion is a brain injury caused by a blow to the head. Concussions can be very serious. Luckily, Alex walked away from the hospital a few days later, with only a few bruises on his head, a cast on his broken arm, and a very angry mom.

Alex didn't take the dangers of the road seriously and let his feelings get in the way of making safe choices. By lying to his mom and thinking he knew better, he put himself in serious danger. "You could have been killed," his mom screamed on the car ride home from the hospital. Alex was sad and angry at himself for being so careless. And he knew deep down that she was right.

Words to Know

public: Open to anyone.
intersections: Places where two streets cross, usually with a stop sign or red light.
distracted: Having your attention pulled away from what you should be focusing on.
passengers: People in a car other than the driver.

Chapter Two

What Makes the Road a Dangerous Place?

Rachel Borofsky is a city crossing guard. A crossing guard is someone who works for a city's or town's government to direct traffic. They make sure that people, especially young people, cross the road safely. She has been working as a crossing guard for almost twenty-five years. She has worked in both cities and suburban towns. Having worked as a crossing guard for so many years, Rachel has seen many accidents. Her job is to make the road a safer place, and she does the best she can. It is a job that has made her understand all too well just how dangerous the road can be.

THE DANGERS OF SUBURBAN ROADS

Rachel began her career as a crossing guard working in a suburban town. She took the job after her daughter was almost killed in a car accident. A car was making a quick right turn when her daughter, Brittany, was trying to cross the street. Brittany looked both ways, but the car was in a big hurry and turned when she was already in the street. Rachel says accidents like this and Alex's accident from chapter 1 are very common on suburban roads.

Riding the school bus can be the safest way to get to and from school, but the bus has its own risks and you still need to be careful around it.

How Drunk Driving Makes the Roads Even More Dangerous

Drinking affects a person's driving in many ways. These include blurry vision, slowed reaction time, falling asleep at the wheel, difficulty doing a few things at once (such as staying in a lane while paying attention to the other cars on the road), failure to obey road rules, and taking more risks than usual. One of the most noticeable signs of drunk drivers is a car swerving on the road for no reason. Staying aware of drunk or distracted drivers is an important part of road safety!

"A big reason for this is that most suburban roads don't have sidewalks," Rachel explains. This means that when young people in the suburbs want to travel from one place to another, they have to walk on or very near the roads. Some young people are so used to using roads like this that they become careless around them. "I used to see young people in the suburbs making careless decisions every day," Rachel says. "They didn't even know how much danger they were putting themselves in."

There are also fewer forms of **public** transportation than in the city. Public transportation is any form of travel, like buses and trains, that people share without making arrangements ahead of time. "Buses are usually made available in the suburbs to take kids to and from school," Rachel says, "and riding the bus is certainly the safest way to get to school." But she is also quick to point out that buses are not without their own dangers.

A young person is far more likely to be hurt trying to get on or off a bus than by actually riding on one. Imagine a young person getting off of a bus holding a very important assignment from one of his teachers. The assignment slips out of his hands and falls under the bus. Without thinking, the young man crouches under the bus to try and save the important assignment. Thinking everyone has gotten off the bus safely and unable to see the boy in his mirrors, the bus driver begins to drive away. Sadly, accidents like these can be deadly.

"Most young people have to go through bus safety courses at school," Rachel says, "and a good bus driver will enforce the rules that kids learn during these courses." These rules save many lives. But rules can only do so much to protect young people from careless drivers. "Many suburban drivers really have no idea how dangerous driving past a bus at a bus stop can be," says Rachel. Buses are so big that a car can't see someone who is trying to cross the street until they are already in the path of the car. It is illegal for a car to pass a school bus as it is picking kids up or dropping them off. "But despite these laws," Rachel continues, "there are a lot of careless drivers in the suburbs and accidents still happen."

As Rachel pointed out, the carelessness of people walking on streets isn't the only reason roads are so dangerous. Careless drivers are far more dangerous than people walking. Drivers like these are another reason understanding road safety is so important. "Drivers are supposed to drive below the speed limit and be extra careful of people crossing the street and at **intersections**," Rachel says, mentioning her daughter's accident. Intersections can be especially dangerous, because

Many cities have sidewalks or other areas to walk that are safe from cars. Since suburban areas are usually just designed for cars, they often don't have sidewalks—and they can be more dangerous for pedestrians.

Road Safety

a driver making a turn often won't be able to see someone walking until it is too late. But accidents like these are caused only in part by careless driving.

"Many [more] accidents happen because a driver simply isn't paying attention," Rachel says, mentioning how many times she was almost hit by cars, because the drivers were **distracted**. "There are so many distractions that today's drivers have to deal with," Rachel continues. Cell phones, loud music, **passengers**, and even just thinking about something other than driving can cause a driver to become distracted. "Someone crossing the street may think that an oncoming car sees them," Rachel says. "But unless you make eye contact with the driver and they wave for you to cross, they probably don't even know that you are there."

Then there is the biggest distraction of all: drunk drivers. According to Rachel, hundreds of kids are killed a year due to drunk driving accidents. And according to MADD (Mothers Against Drunk Driving), well over one million drivers a year are arrested for drunk driving in America alone.

THE DANGERS OF CITY ROADS

City roads are both very similar and very different from suburban roads. "[Young people] still need to be aware of reckless driving, drunk driving, and need to be careful when crossing a busy street," Rachel says. "But after working in a city, I would say that cities are actually a little safer than suburban streets."

A big difference between city streets and suburban roads is that city streets have sidewalks, which keep people off the street and out of the way of cars. And most intersections have signals that let walkers know when it is safe to cross. This means that even though there are more cars and more people walking, there are also more ways to keep these people safe.

Of course, not following these rules or obeying signals can be extremely dangerous. "Many people in the city think that looking both ways is enough to keep them safe from oncoming traffic," Rachel says. According to her, this can be a big mistake. "City drivers don't expect that there will be anyone in the road when they have a green light ahead of them." City streets are also a lot smaller and are driven by many more cars than suburban roads. There are a lot of things that a city driver needs to be aware of besides people crossing the street illegally.

"While walking a city street can be pretty safe," Rachel says, "riding a bike is another story." There are more cyclists than ever in the city. One reason for this is that "people today are more worried than ever about environmental issues," Rachel says. "And this has led to a lot more people buying and riding bikes." Many cities are even beginning to install bike rental services right on the street.

"If you don't own a bike in the city, then you probably aren't very used to riding a bike in the city," Rachel says. People who have never ridden a bike in the city need to take it very slow at first. They need to get used to biking next to traffic and need to stay aware of the dangers the city has to offer. At first, they should probably also follow behind someone who has some experience riding around the city.

Like Alex in chapter 1, many cyclists don't realize that they are supposed to follow the same

Bike rentals are great for the environment and help people stay healthy, but more people riding bikes means there are more bike accidents!

24

Road Safety

City Bike Rentals

Bike rental services let someone quickly rent a bike from one location and drop it off at another. These bike rental services are great for the environment and push people to exercise more. But they are also part of the reason cities are seeing more and more traffic accidents involving cyclists. In almost every major city, there are now more than one thousand traffic accidents involving bicyclists each year.

rules of the road as cars and other vehicles. They have to stop at red lights and stop signs. And using hand signals in the city is even more important than in the suburbs.

Many cities have installed bike lanes on the roads. These bike lanes are between the lanes of cars and the parking spots, all the way to the right of the road. These bike lanes are great, because they keep cyclists out of the way of traffic. But they also create a new danger for cyclists. Most bike accidents in cities are caused by car doors opening in the way of cyclists.

Words to Know

community: The people around you, in your family, school, or town.
defensive: Taking action to protect yourself.
sobriety: Being free of drugs and alcohol.
technology: Tools or machines people use to help them do more than they could on their own.

Chapter Three

Staying Safe and Being Prepared

"I spend every day fighting to keep the roads safe," says traffic police officer Sarah Gilmore. In her town, Officer Gilmore is the head of a number of projects to prevent traffic accidents. "A big part of my job is letting people know how dangerous it can be when they aren't safe on our town's roadways." As a traffic police officer, Officer Gilmore sees almost every accident in her town. "It is one thing," she says, "to hear numbers about how many people die in car accidents each year. But it really affects you when you see the faces and families of the victims of these accidents." According to Officer Gilmore, when people are careless and make dangerous decisions, it doesn't only affect them. It affects many people around them. "This is the most important thing to remember," she says, "because it gives a young person a good reason to stay safe."

CROSSING GUARDS AND POLICE OFFICERS

Crossing guards like Rachel from chapter 2 and police officers like Officer Gilmore play important roles in keeping our roads and intersections safe. Crossing guards are placed at busy intersections to prevent the kind of accident that happened to Rachel's daughter, Brittany. Some intersections can be especially dangerous, and crossing guards have prevented many accidents between cars and people crossing the street.

Police officers are especially important. They enforce the rules of the road. "My job is made a

Especially in areas of heavy traffic, a traffic police officer's job is important to keep people safe, whether they're driving, biking, or walking.

Road Safety

lot harder," Officer Gilmore says, "because a lot of young people do not respect rules or the people who enforce them." Like Alex from chapter 1, many people think they know better or that they can stay safe without following all the rules. "It may sound surprising," Office Gilmore says, "but my job as a traffic cop isn't really about keeping people safe. It is about making sure that people keep themselves safe."

LAWS AND THE RULES OF THE ROAD

"The laws that govern our roads are there for a reason," Officer Gilmore continues. "These laws may seem silly to some people who don't know any better. But they are there to keep people safe. If everyone followed the rules and laws, there would still be a few accidents. Some accidents will happen no matter how safe the people involved are being. But trust me, anyone who has been in an accident on the road and comes out alive begins to take traffic laws a lot more seriously."

According to Officer Gilmore, the most important rule to remember is that if a crossing guard or police officer is directing traffic, you must always listen to her. In the city, police officers often direct traffic. Whether you are walking, riding a bike, or driving a car, if a police officer or crossing guard tells you to move or cross the road, you should listen.

Many people think traffic police officers only spend their time pulling over careless drivers and giving them tickets. As a traffic police officer, this is one of Officer Gilmore's duties. But she does much more than that. She works with others in her **community** to start projects about road safety. And she spends a lot of time making sure people walking and riding their bikes are following the rules. "Many people," she says, "think that bad drivers are to blame for how dangerous the roads are. But this is false." The truth, according to Officer Gilmore, is that most traffic accidents are the result of people being careless. "One class," she says, "that many drivers take is called '**defensive** driving.' This class teaches drivers how to avoid accidents by being aware of other people on the road. It teaches that you may be following the rules and laws but other people might not." Officer Gilmore wishes there were classes available for people who want to learn to walk or ride their bikes defensively. "It is not enough to follow the rules yourself," she says. "You also need to be aware of the other people on the road."

A road is a dangerous place and needs to be treated as dangerous. Making sure you are following the rules is a good way to keep other people out of danger. But it won't keep you out of danger. A distracted or drunk driver is dangerous whether you are following the rules or not.

"Luckily, new laws are being created to keep our roads safer," Officer Gilmore says. "There are finally laws against making calls and texting while driving. Most of these laws should have been in place years ago." These laws have been a big help in preventing distracted driving. But laws are not enough, because without our police officers, there would be no one to enforce these laws. "People need to know," Officer Gilmore says, "that driving distracted is illegal and that they will be punished if they are caught."

Sadly, the police can only do so much. Police can't catch everyone who is driving while distracted. And many people who are caught think they weren't doing anything wrong and were being safe. These people sometimes continue their dangerous actions despite being punished. It

Staying Safe and Being Prepared

Someone who has been drinking cannot drive safely. Make sure you never get into a car with a drunk driver, and if possible, don't let that person drive at all!

Road Safety

Friday and Saturday nights are the times when there is the highest chance of drivers being drunk. It is at these times that you need to be the most on the watch for dangerous drivers!

is not the responsibility of a police officer to make sure you follow the rules of the road. It is your responsibility to keep yourself and others safe by following them!

PREVENTING DRUNK DRIVING

Along with new laws to prevent distracted driving, there are also many groups, including the police, working together to prevent drunk driving. As we mentioned in chapter 2, more than a million people are arrested each year for driving drunk. But even though so many arrests are made, many people still drive drunk. Nearly ten thousand people a year die from drunken driving accidents. That means, on average, someone dies in a drunk driving accident every fifty minutes. And there are over two million people in the United States alone who have been arrested for drunk driving three or more times.

Staying Safe and Being Prepared

Police have a device called a breath analyzer, or a "breathalyzer," that can tell how much alcohol is in a person's blood.

Peer Pressure

"One reason why young people drink and drive dangerously is called peer pressure," says Officer Gilmore. Peer pressure is when others influence our decisions. Part of Officer Gilmore's job is to make young people aware of when they are being affected by peer pressure. A study measured how teens drive when others were in the car. The study showed that teens drove more dangerously when other teens were in the car. A big part of peer pressure is the desire to impress friends. "But drinking and driving is not impressive," Officer Gilmore says. "It only makes our roads very dangerous."

MADD is one of the many groups that Officer Gilmore works with on plans to stop drunk driving. MADD's Campaign to Eliminate Drunk Driving has three steps, which are all very important.

They call the first step "Supporting Our Heroes." This means supporting the brave men and women, like Officer Gilmore, who protect our roads every day. They work long hours, dealing with difficult situations. They often put themselves in danger. Each year, many officers lose their lives in the line of duty. And some of those officers die because of traffic accidents, showing that the roads are unsafe even for the people who try to protect them.

One way that MADD supports police officers is by pushing them to take more action to prevent drunk driving before any accidents happen. One action police officers can take is called a "**sobriety** checkpoint." Drivers are stopped at busy intersections and quickly tested to see if they have been drinking. "In areas where police set up sobriety checkpoints," Officer Gilmore says, "there are a lot less drunk driving accidents." And one way MADD supports police officers is by getting the word out about how well sobriety checkpoints work.

The second way MADD helps prevent drunk driving is called "Sober to Start." "Most people who are arrested for drunk driving," Officer Gilmore says, "have driven drunk many times before actually getting arrested." And each year, many people have their licenses taken away because of being caught drinking and driving too many times. MADD points out that taking away a person's license doesn't work very well, because many of these people continue to drive. MADD is pressuring our government to let these people keep their licenses. Instead of taking licenses, MADD wants to have a device installed in their cars. This device measures how much a person has been drinking before letting him start his car. Thanks to MADD, over twenty states require these devices in people's cars if they are caught drinking and driving even one time.

"Secure Our Future" is the third way MADD is trying to prevent drinking and driving. MADD supports a group of scientists working on technology that would test anyone who climbs into the driver's seat of a car. This technology would stop a car from turning on if the driver is drunk. This **technology** isn't far from being finished. But the fight won't end there. There would have to be laws requiring this technology in every new car sold in America.

Since MADD started in 1980, deaths resulting from drunk driving have been cut in half. This is good, but there's still a long way to go toward preventing drunk driving!

Road Safety

"Drunk driving," Officer Gilmore says, "is the biggest danger that anyone faces on the roads today." And as a mother, Officer Gilmore is happy to be a part of MADD, people doing their best to stop drunk driving once and for all. "Imagine knowing that every driver of every car on the road was sober," she says. "That is the kind of world I want my kids to live in. Groups like MADD are making that possible."

Staying Safe and Being Prepared

Words to Know

professionally: For a living or for a job.

Chapter Four

What Can You Do to Stay Safe?

Professional driver and parent Christian Valencia drives people all over the country. He needs to be very safe when he drives. If Christian were to get into any kind of accident, whether it was his fault or not, the company he works for would be very angry. This means Christian needs to be much more careful than most drivers. In the ten years that he has been driving **professionally**, Christian is happy to say he has never gotten into an accident. But there have been many times that he has come close. In a few of these close calls, Christian has almost gotten into accidents with young people. Because he needs to be so careful when he drives, he knows a lot about staying safe on the road. "There is a lot that young people can do to stay safe on the roads," he says, "both in a car and out."

STAYING SAFE IN THE CAR

Christian loves young people. He has three children he couldn't be more proud of. But as a driver, Christian is always nervous of having to drive young people.

"Kids can be a big distraction on the road," Christian says. "Sometimes they will refuse to wear their seat belts. Sometimes their parents even say 'It's okay' if they don't want to wear it. I have to explain to them that it is not only unsafe but if we were pulled over by a police officer, I could get

Seat belts are the best way to keep from getting hurt if you get into an accident. Get in the habit of buckling up!

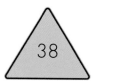

38   **Road Safety**

In order to drive safely, drivers need to pay attention to many different things. When you're riding in a car, make sure you don't distract the driver.

a ticket." Christian is right. Not wearing a seat belt is extremely dangerous. Most people killed in car accidents every year were not wearing their seat belts. "Many children think that wearing a seatbelt is annoying or unneeded," Christian says.

The truth is that seat belts save nearly ten thousand lives a year. But still, not everyone wears a seat belt. In fact, one study showed that if everyone wore a seat belt, over five thousand more lives would be saved a year, and over one hundred thousand injuries would be prevented. "When it comes to keeping yourself safe in a car," Christian says, "your seatbelt is your best bet."

Christian also says young people can be a big distraction while he drives. "Most young people have never driven a car before," he says, "so they have no idea of how many things we drivers need to be aware of. They do not understand that by being a distraction, they are putting me, themselves, and their families at risk." According to Christian, one of the best ways for young people to stay safe in a car is to make sure they are not distracting the driver. "But children aren't the only

What Can You Do to Stay Safe?

Being in the road can be dangerous even if it's in a designated crosswalk. Pay attention and make sure that no cars are coming before you step into the road.

Road Safety

people who can be distracting. Some of their parents can be much worse. On a perfect day of driving," Christian laughs, "all the parents and children that I drove would be asleep."

This, of course, is not possible. And Christian understands why kids would sometimes be a distraction. "Long car rides are boring," Christian says, "and when a young person is bored, they can turn into a big distraction. I am fine if a kid has some questions about the car or wants to talk a little. But some kids scream or complain and others unbuckle their seatbelts halfway through a trip." Christian says that the least distracting young people he drives are well behaved and quiet. Many of them have brought something with them, like video games or a book, to entertain themselves. "[Young people] need to remember," he says, "that when they are distracting a driver, they are putting themselves in serious danger. If I cannot be fully aware on the road, I cannot protect them from accidents and bad drivers."

STAYING AWARE ON THE STREET

"I have had too many close-calls," Christian says, "with young people who aren't being aware near streets." According to Christian, this is a much bigger problem in the suburbs than in the city. "In the suburbs," he says, "kids are constantly out on the street. They walk, play, and ride bikes there. And it can be very dangerous!"

In one of these near misses, Christian says some young people were playing baseball in their yard. One kid hit the ball out into the street. Another, wanting to get the ball quickly to throw it back, ran right out in front of his car without even looking to see if it was safe. "She was lucky," he says, "because if I had been distracted or speeding, I would have hit her head on." Young people need to be extra careful anywhere near roads, especially roads where the speed limit is more than 30 miles per hour. The chances of being killed by a car are much higher if the car is going 40 miles per hour than if the car was going 30 miles per hour. Most suburban streets have a 30-mile-per-hour speed limit, but this doesn't stop people from speeding down these streets. Luckily, the engines in the cars of people who are speeding often make a lot of noise.

When nearing a street, a young person should follow three rules: stop, look, and listen. Stop so that you don't step out in front of oncoming traffic. Look so that you can see if there are any cars coming. And listen, because sometimes you can hear traffic before you can see it, especially when someone is speeding.

"Kids also need to understand that roads are far more dangerous at night," Christian says. Bikes have to have four reflectors on them at all times. And many bikes do not have enough reflectors. But the real danger is when people walk around at night. Most clothes are not shiny at all. Being aware of cars on the street means doing everything you can to make sure drivers are aware of you. Anyone walking around at night should wear a reflective vest, glove, hat, or armband, so she can be better seen by the traffic around her.

FOLLOWING THE RULES OF THE ROAD

We mentioned some of the rules of the road in chapter 1. When walking or riding your bike on or near a street, following these rules is the best way to keep you and others safe.

Drivers often slow down at street corners, and they know to watch for pedestrians there, so corners are the safest place to cross the road.

Road Safety

Some Roads Are More Dangerous Than Others

Being aware near roads at all times is an important part of staying safe. But it also helps to know which roads are more dangerous than others. Some roads are more dangerous because of the way they are built. Some local governments are now studying which are the most dangerous roads for people walking and for cyclists. They are posting signs near these roads to let walkers and cyclists know to watch out. Knowing which roads to watch out for, regardless of signs, will help anyone stay safe when they are traveling on these roads. Many of these studies are now available online. Look up your area to see which roads you should stay away from and be extra careful around.

The rules for walking on or near a road are simple and many of them we have already mentioned:

- Always cross at corners and within marked crosswalks where available.
- If crossing anywhere other than a corner, always let any cars or trucks go by first.
- Stop, look, and listen. When looking, look left, right, and left again before crossing. And watch for turning cars.
- Always walk on the left side of the road.
- If there is no sidewalk on the road, walk as far off the road as possible.
- Use the buddy system. Walk and cross with others when possible.
- Obey traffic signals, especially Walk/Don't Walk.
- Be aware! Don't think cars are going to stop for you. Make eye contact with the driver to make sure that she sees you.
- Wear reflective clothing when walking at night.

According to Christian, if everyone followed these rules, he would have a much easier time driving and wouldn't have to worry so much about getting into accidents. "But people on bicycles," Christian says, "are a much bigger worry for me. These people very rarely follow any of the rules that they are supposed to follow." The rules of the road for a bike rider are simple too:

- Before riding, make sure your tires have air and your brakes are working properly.
- Wear a helmet, and wear it properly.
- Use hand signals when making a turn, slowing down, or stopping.
- If you need to carry something, bring a backpack. Do not carry anything in your hands.
- Don't wear headphones.
- Don't ride on any roads that are closed to bicycles, such as highways.
- Always stop at stop signs and red lights.
- Use the bike lane if there is one.
- If there isn't a bike lane, ride on the right side of the road, as far over as possible.
- Never ride on the sidewalk in a city unless you absolutely have to.

What Can You Do to Stay Safe?

Whether you're walking, biking, or driving, make sure you respect the dangers of the road and do your best to keep yourself and others safe!

44

Road Safety

- Make sure your bike has four reflectors: one on the front, one on the back, and one on each wheel. Consider getting a headlight for your bicycle to make it easier for drivers to see you.
- Never let a friend ride on your bike's pegs or handlebars.
- If you are riding with a friend, bike next to each other. But never let more than two people ride next to each other on a road.

We need to respect our roads. They are dangerous for many reasons. And the rules of the road for cyclists, drivers, and people walking were made so none of us will get in each other's way. If we all follow these rules, we can leave our homes every day, trusting that no matter where we go or how we get there, we will make it home safe and sound.

Find Out More

ONLINE

Bike Safety
kidshealth.org/kid/watch/out/bike_safety.html

Kids and Bicycle Safety
www.nhtsa.gov/people/injury/pedbimot/bike/kidsandbikesafetyweb

National Highway Traffic Safety Administration
www.nhtsa.gov

Make Roads Safe
www.makeroadssafe.org

Traffic Safety Kids Page
www.safeny.ny.gov/kids.htm

IN BOOKS

Apelqvist, Eva. *Getting Ready to Drive: A How-to Guide (Life: A How-to Guide)*. Berkeley Heights, N.J.: Enslow, 2011.

Hartley, Diana. *Road Safety*. New York: McGraw-Hill, 2009.

Gordon, Mike, and Claire Llewellyn. *Watch Out! On the Road*. Hauppauge, N.Y.: Barron's Educational Series, 2006.

Raatma, Lucia. *Bicycle Safety (Living Well)*. North Mankato, Minn.: Child's World, 2003.

Index

About the Author & Consultant

Christie Marlowe was raised in New York City where she lives with her husband and works as a writer, journalist, and web designer.

Dr. Ronald D. Stephens currently serves as executive director of the National School Safety Center. His past experience includes service as a teacher, assistant superintendent, and school board member. Administrative experience includes serving as a chief school business officer, with responsibilities over school safety and security, and as vice president of Pepperdine University.

Dr. Stephens has conducted more than 1000 school security and safety site assessments throughout the United States. He was described by the *Denver Post* as "the nation's leading school crime prevention expert." Dr. Stephens serves as consultant and frequent speaker for school districts, law enforcement agencies and professional organizations worldwide. He is the author of numerous articles on school safety as well as the author of *School Safety: A Handbook for Violence Prevention*. His career is distinguished by military service. He is married and has three children.

Picture Credits

Dreamstime.com:
    8: Mikael Damkier
    11: Tepic
    12: Sean Pavone
    13: Wessel Du Plooy
    14: Anskuw
    16: Krisgun01
    18: Glenda Powers
    20: Blueelephant
    22: Hupeng
    24: Bambi L. Dingman
    26: Chhobi
    28: Lee Snider

    30: Ghubonamin
    31: Haraldmuc
    32: Ronalds Stikans
    34: Dmitriy Melnikov
    36: Mauricio Jordan De Souza Coelho
    38: Andres Rodriguez
    39: Lisa F. Young
    40: Photographerlondon
    42: James Crawford

Fotolia.com:
    10: Lucky Dragon
    44: Maridav